P9-BEE-540

JIMMIE JOHNSON

RACE CAR LEGENDS

COLLECTOR'S EDITION

JIMMIE JOHNSON

Bill Fleischman

CHELSEA HOUSE
PUBLISHERS

Cover Photo: Jimmie Johnson stands by his No. 48 Chevrolet prior to a practice run at the Daytona International Speedway in Daytona Beach, Florida in July 2004.

CHELSEA HOUSE PUBLISHERS

VP, New Product Development   Sally Cheney
Director of Production   Kim Shinners
Creative Manager   Takeshi Takahashi
Manufacturing Manager   Diann Grasse

STAFF FOR JIMMIE JOHNSON

Editorial Assistant Sarah Sharpless
Production Editor Bonnie Cohen
Photo Editor Pat Holl
Series Design and Layout Hierophant Publishing Services/EON PreMedia

http://www.chelseahouse.com

First Printing

1   3   5   7   9   8   6   4   2

Library of Congress Cataloging-in-Publication Data

Fleischman, Bill.
    Jimmie Johnson / Bill Fleischman.
        p. cm.—(Race car legends. Collector's edition)
    Includes bibliographical references and index.
    ISBN 0-7910-8672-0
    1. Johnson, Jimmie, 1975—Juvenile literature. 2. Automobile racing drivers—United States—Biography—Juvenile literature. I. Title. II. Series.
GV1032.J54F54 2005
796.72'092—dc22

2005011368

All links and Web addresses were checked and verified to be correct at the time of publication. Because of the dynamic nature of the Web, some addresses and links may have changed since publication and may no longer be valid.

TABLE OF CONTENTS

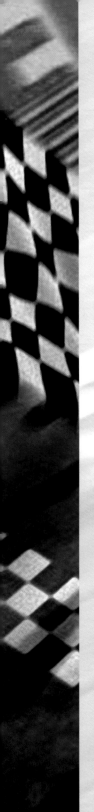

"THE WORST TRAGEDY IN MOTORSPORTS"

All the drivers in the National Association for Stock Car Racing's elite Nextel Cup series are superb at what they do. They drive stock cars fast, at 180 to 190 miles per hour on superspeedways. Often, the cars are only a hand's width apart. One hiccup, one lapse of concentration, and the smoke and sound of screeching metal will signify a crash. Sometimes, what sets these drivers apart is how they handle setbacks. There are tough losses, where frequently another driver's mistake costs them a victory. But the toughest situation of all is the loss of people they care about.

Jimmie Johnson stepped up big time in the fall of 2004. While Johnson and his Hendrick Motorsports teammates Jeff Gordon, Terry Labonte, and Brian Vickers were racing at Martinsville Speedway, they did not know that a plane carrying the Hendrick family and personnel had crashed into a mountain near the historic race track in south-central Virginia. Among those who perished in the crash were owner Rick Hendrick's only son, Ricky; Rick's brother, John; and John's 22-year-old twin daughters, Kimberly and Jennifer. The crash also killed Randy Dorton, the chief engine builder

Members of Jimmie Johnson's pit crew react to news that Hendrick family members and personnel perished in a plane crash. NASCAR officials informed a stunned Jimmie Johnson immediately after he won the Subway 500 stock car race at Martinsville Speedway, October 24, 2004.

for Hendrick Motorsports, and the company's general manager, Jeff Turner.

"It's probably the worst tragedy that's ever happened in motorsports," said Max Muhleman, a Charlotte, North Carolina-based sports marketing executive.[1]

Johnson and the other drivers did not learn about the plane crash until Johnson had won. A stunned Johnson was escorted to a NASCAR trailer where officials informed him of the crash. There was no victory celebration following the race and no meeting with the media.

Grieving Hendrick personnel at the track hugged each other and prayed as their tears flowed. Hearts were broken, but they carried on because racing is what they do, and they knew that the victims and team owner Rick Hendrick would want them to carry on.

Five days later, on qualifying day for the race at Atlanta Motor Speedway, the Hendrick drivers and crew chiefs held a press conference. None of them wanted to be there. Their eyes, and sad expressions confirmed that they were all still hurting. But they knew it was their duty to the fans and media to express their thoughts and emotions. All the drivers and crew chiefs conveyed a sense of dignity throughout the press conference.

Vickers, who turned 21 years old on the day of the crash, sat on a stool in the front row. He spoke first and did not take questions.

Ricky Hendrick had pushed his father to hire Vickers, then in his late teens, to drive in the NASCAR Busch Grand National series, the "prep school" for the NASCAR Nextel Cup series (known as the Winston Cup series from 1971–2003). When it was Johnson's turn, he spoke from the heart:

> The truth of the matter is that the week has gone by, and here we are at the race track, and we have to get to work and try to get through it. That doesn't mean that the grieving is not going to continue, [and] the pain, especially for the families. We're all going through a lot of pain, and we're friends. There are a lot of family members who are experiencing pain that a lot of us will never understand.
>
> We're definitely going to put that effort forth [to win], but it's so overwhelming. It's just going to take time. It's hard to know how to feel, what to think, how to do it, but we just all feel so sorry for the families. All of us are going through a lot of pain, but most of all we feel sorry for all the families involved.[2]

On June 2, 2002, Johnson won the NASCAR Cup Series race at Dover International Speedway in Delaware. He swept two races at Dover during his rookie year, after winning his first race in California.

Johnson, 29 years old, exhibited a maturity that some people 10 years older than he might not have been able to show. In fact, the composure he displayed was similar to the way he races: Johnson is very smooth and consistent on the race track. Two days after the press conference, Johnson won a race in Atlanta, Georgia. The victory somewhat lightened the mood around the race track and put smiles on peoples' faces, especially those at Hendrick Motorsports. In a tribute to Ricky Hendrick, Johnson and the other smiling Hendrick drivers wore their caps backwards, as Ricky had always worn his. It was clear that teammates Gordon, Labonte, and Vickers were happy for Johnson.

Pit crew members service the No. 48 Lowe's Chevrolet, driven by Jimmie Johnson. The speed and efficiency of the pit crew can make the critical difference in the outcome of a race.

Although 2004 was only Johnson's third full season racing in the Cup series, his stature in NASCAR has quickly risen. He finished in fifth place in the points standings in his rookie year in 2002, winning three races. He swept the two races at Dover International Speedway in Delaware after winning his first race at California Speedway in Sears Point. The following year, Johnson was runner-up in points while again winning three races: at Lowe's Motor Speedway near Charlotte, North Carolina, and a sweep of the two races in New Hampshire. It is very difficult to win in the 36-race Cup series. Most drivers consider winning two or three races a year a job well done.

Forty-three cars start each race. The cars at the front of the field are usually separated by tenths or hundredths of a second, meaning they are fast. Over the duration of a race, which lasts three hours or more, the drivers who can handle the race track while avoiding crashes and receiving quick work by their crews during pit stops are the ones who finish up front.

The 2004 season was even more successful for Johnson, proving that the experience he was gaining was paying off. Driving the blue No. 48 Lowe's Chevrolet again, he won a series-leading eight races. Included in Johnson's collection of victories were sweeps at Pocono Raceway in Pennsylvania, Darlington Raceway in South Carolina, and Lowe's Motor Speedway in North Carolina.

Perhaps the most impressive portion of Johnson's 2004 season was during the Chase for the Championship. For the 2004 season, NASCAR introduced a new format to decide the Cup points champion. After the first 26 races, the points slate for the top 10 drivers was erased. To start the final 10-race "Chase," the top drivers were separated by just five points each. Scoring for the final 10 races was then conducted under the regular system, with 190 points being the greatest number of points a driver could earn per race.

The goal of this change was to create more interest in the Cup series during the fall, when NASCAR is competing for attention with the major league baseball playoffs and World Series, the National Football League, and college football. In many previous seasons, the leading driver would gain such a large points advantage that some fans would lose interest in the series. That did not happen during the '04 Chase. The new points system proved to be even more successful than NASCAR had imagined.

Following a disappointing start in the Chase, Johnson wound up as a major player. Four races into the Chase, Johnson was 247 points out of first, in ninth place.

He rebounded to win at Lowe's Motor Speedway, then won the next two races at Martinsville Speedway and Atlanta Motor Speedway. Suddenly, he was runner-up to leader Kurt Busch, just 59 points off the pace. A sixth-place finish in the next race at Phoenix International Raceway in Arizona dropped him to fourth place. But he was only 48 points out of first place. Johnson won again at Darlington Raceway, and then, with only one race in the Chase remaining, he was just 18 points behind Busch.

Prior to the season finale at Homestead-Miami Speedway in Florida, Johnson was not the only driver in contention for the championship. Jeff Gordon trailed Busch by 21 points. Completing the top five were Dale Earnhardt Jr., 72 points behind Busch's, and Mark Martin, 82 points out of first place.

With Busch, Johnson, and Gordon all having a chance for the title, the atmosphere before the race was electric. Busch showed that he would be tough to beat when he won the pole position with a time of 179.319 miles per hour. Johnson stumbled in qualifying and had to start 39th.

Early in the race, Johnson managed to avoid collisions and gradually moved toward the front. Near the end of the race, the three contenders were running in the top 10.

Greg Biffle, a Roush Racing teammate of Busch, won the race. Johnson came in second, Gordon finished third, and Busch ended in fifth place. Busch won his first championship by a mere eight points over Johnson. Gordon was 16 points behind Busch.

After his second consecutive runner-up finish in the standings, Johnson said:

> We're definitely disappointed that we didn't win the championship. But if you look back four or five weeks ago, we weren't even in the Chase. With the loss of so many people in the [plane crash] tragedy, it's amazing

that we were able to have the finish that we did. It was an incredible season for this Lowe's team. We won a lot of races. That's something I'm very proud of. I set a personal goal to try to win five races this year. To have eight, and four in the Chase, is pretty amazing.[3]

It is interesting that Johnson was not initially a fan of the new points system. Although he is a young driver, Johnson is a traditionalist. "I don't think the new rules really show who the true champion is or will be," the Californian said earlier in the 2004 season.

This is about 36 races, it's about endurance, showing consistency, and I think our point system should reflect that. The [new] system is for entertainment. It's TV-based, not competition-based. I don't think it's fair if Dale [Earnhardt] Jr. has a 300-point lead and he goes into race 27 and it's [only] a five-point lead.[4]

Following the season-ending race, Johnson had changed his mind:

I think it's turned out to be a good battle. You have the 97 [car, Kurt Busch] who was relatively consistent the whole stretch. Then you have us with a couple bad races and a bunch of wins and we were able to get back in the middle of it. The top five guys don't have to worry about points like they did in the past. This year you didn't have the year-long stress to worry about. With all the excitement we had built around this race there are more positives than negatives with this points system. I think that, in the end, it will be better for everybody.

Johnson still thinks that race winners should receive more for their effort. "I've been a fan of raising the difference in the points all along," he said.[5] Johnson thinks giving race winners a larger distribution of points would stimulate better racing. Johnson's comments about the new points system reflect his willingness to speak out on racing issues.

Johnson is an important figure in NASCAR's new generation. With veteran drivers like Mark Martin, Dale Jarrett, Rusty Wallace, Terry Labonte, and Bill Elliott nearing the end of their careers, drivers such as Jimmie Johnson, Kurt Busch, Dale Earnhardt Jr., Jeff Gordon, Tony Stewart, Ryan Newman, and Matt Kenseth will be carrying on the tradition that has made NASCAR racing so popular throughout the United States.

As the 2005 season began, Johnson was the favorite in many preseason polls for the championship. The fans based their predictions on his strong finish in 2004 and his two previous runner-up finishes. Johnson's crew chief, Chad Knaus, is considered one of the best in NASCAR. Johnson's driving style is also an asset. While he is aggressive, as all good racers must be, he is not out of control. "I try to race everybody

DID YOU KNOW?

Jimmie Johnson explains how drivers perform "burnouts" after winning races:

"On the cool-down lap, there's a brake adjuster in the car and you adjust it so that you can hold the car and really get the tires smoking good. You just rev it [the engine] up, dump the clutch, put your left foot on the brake and your right foot on the gas and get 'em [the tires] boiling."*

*Jimmie Johnson, press conference, Atlanta Motor Speedway, October 21, 2003.

how they race me," he said. "I try to respect everyone on the racetrack. I don't try to put anyone in a bad situation. Patience means more than anything."[6]

In the season-opening Daytona 500, Johnson was racing to win. He and teammate Jeff Gordon battled Tony Stewart, Dale Earnhardt Jr., and reigning Cup champion Kurt Busch in the closing laps. When a caution flag was waved on lap 199 of the scheduled 200-lap race, NASCAR used its green/white/checkered rule. Because NASCAR and fans want races to end under green flag conditions, races are extended two laps. The field gets a green flag to resume the race, then the white flag signifying the last lap and then the checkered flag to indicate the winner. On the final lap, racing at top speed, Johnson and Stewart's cars scraped each other. As they crossed the start/finish line with Gordon winning, Stewart slid his orange Chevrolet into Johnson's Chevy. As the cars slowed, Johnson banged Stewart back.

Stewart was upset because he failed to win after dominating the race: he led the most laps (107 of 203). Both drivers were summoned to the NASCAR trailer for a "discussion" of the incidents. After the race Johnson and Stewart said there were no hard feelings. Referring to the mobile office where NASCAR officials work at races, Johnson said, "Two trips to the truck is rare for me. But I'm going to stand my ground when someone leans on me."[7]

2

FROM OFF-ROAD
TO BUSCH GRAND
NATIONAL

Jimmie Johnson was born September 17, 1975. He grew up
in El Cajon, California, near San Diego. He has two younger
brothers, Jarit and Jessie. Their father, Gary, operated a
backhoe on construction jobs. Their mother, Cathy, drove a
school bus. The family spent many weekends camping in the
desert. The boys also raced motorcycles. When Jimmie was
five years old, he rode a "pee wee" motorcycle (top speed,
5 miles per hour). Later, he raced dirt motorcycles. These
vehicles can be dangerous, because dirt racing involves riding off steep jumps. Unlike some parents, Gary Johnson says
he never pressured his sons when they were racing. He just
wanted them to have fun. When Jimmie was a teenager, he
started racing off-road buggies. When he was in high school
his parents insisted that he maintain a B average in order to
continue racing.

During a 1995 off-road race on the Baja Peninsula in
Mexico, Johnson and a teammate crashed. "I'd been driving
for 20 hours then, hadn't slept, so I dozed off a little bit,"

he recalled. "I drove into a rain storm that woke me up." (The off-road vehicles don't have windshields.) "I was coming up on a turn [and] was going way too fast. I tried to get it slowed down, but I knew I was going off road, so I figured I better go off straight." Johnson said he hit a rock "the size of a Volkswagen" and flipped. Johnson says there were "about 100 Mexicans at the bottom of this wash, with bonfires and their wives, watching the race."

Jessie Johnson, younger brother of Jimmie, is part of the Johnson family racing tradition.

He spent almost two days with the Mexicans, waiting for people from the race to find them. Johnson does not speak Spanish and the Mexicans did not speak English. "We just sat there staring at each other for a couple of days," he said. "We could hear the other competitors driving nearby, but I guess they didn't see us."[8]

In 1999, the entire Johnson family moved to North Carolina. Gary drives Johnson's motor home to races. "It was hard to pick up and leave," Cathy Johnson said. "We had always lived in California. But family is what's most important."[9] Johnson's brothers, Jarit and Jessie, also are involved in racing. They appear with him in a Levi Strauss advertising campaign.

Johnson's father was a mechanic for a driver who raced a buggy in the Mickey Thompson Stadium Off-Road series. When Jimmie was 15 years old, he started racing in the Superlites class. A year later, Chevrolet chose him to race a truck in the Stadium Off-Road series. Herb Fishel, an influential executive in Chevrolet's racing program, spotted Johnson. Johnson said: "With my upbringing and background, there's been a few people who have made [racing success] possible, and Herb's one of them. If he hadn't, I'd still be sitting in El Cajon, doing what everybody else I graduated high school with is doing."[10]

When he was racing stadium trucks, Johnson wasn't sure how far he would go in the sport. "When I got into stadium trucks," he said, "I tore up plenty of equipment and drove [team owner] Jon Nelson crazy. But I learned some hard lessons through that." What Johnson learned was his driving "style." He knew if he continued to wreck his equipment, he would not get rides. "But at the same time," he said, "I had to go out there and be fast and show that I have potential and can win races. So I've been able to adapt to a certain style: to push when I need to race hard, but at the same time not take unnecessary risks."[11] Johnson credits Rick Johnson, a former Supercross champion, with helping him develop his racing style.

In 1998, when he was 23 years old, Johnson started racing the American Speed Association (ASA) Stock Car series. Such NASCAR stars as Mark Martin, Rusty Wallace, and the late Alan Kulwicki, the 1992 Cup champion, prepped in ASA. Johnson won ASA Rookie of the Year honors in 1998. He followed his impressive first season by finishing third in the 1999 ASA points standings.

From 1999 through 2001, Johnson raced in the NASCAR Busch Grand National series. Drivers in the Busch series, as it is known, generally fall into two categories. They are either promising younger drivers on their way to the Cup series or regular Busch drivers who don't expect to make it to Cup. In

Jimmie Johnson won his first Busch Grand National race at the Chicagoland Speedway in Joliet, Illinois, on July 14, 2001.

1999, Johnson appeared in just five Busch Grand National races with one top-10 finish. The following year he was a full-time Busch Grand National racer, finishing 10th in the points standings. He had six top-10 finishes, but no wins. In 2001, driving again for Herzog Motorsports, he won his first

Busch Grand National race at Chicagoland Speedway. He completed the season in eighth place in the standings.

Johnson's record is proof that a driver doesn't have to win a lot of races to be noticed by team owners in the Cup series. Rick Hendrick liked Johnson's potential in the American Speed Association (ASA) series. After a couple full seasons on the Busch circuit, Hendrick figured that Johnson was ready to move up. During 2001 Johnson made his Cup series debut, appearing in three races for Hendrick Motorsports. His best finish was 25th in the season's final race at Homestead, Florida. He said:

> I figured that I needed to be dominating in the Busch series to even be recognized by a Cup team. In my first season in Busch, I hadn't even finished in the top five yet when Jeff [Gordon] and [team owner] Rick Hendrick were talking about me driving a Cup car. I thought there was no way. What did they see? I have so much to learn.[12]

Did you know? Jimmie Johnson's parents required that he maintain a B average in high school if he wanted to continue racing. Referring to Johnson's parents, Gary and Cathy, teammate Jeff Gordon says, "I think they disciplined him while he was coming up through racing to respect others and work hard."

3

ROOKIE WITH THE RIGHT TEAM

Johnson caught everyone's attention at the start of the 2002 Cup season by winning the pole for the Daytona 500 with a speed of 185.831 miles per hour. It's almost unheard of for a rookie to be the fastest qualifier for the Daytona 500, but Johnson did it. Afterward, he spread the credit around, saying, "This is unbelievable. You always think you have the ability to come out here and be competitive, but you just don't know until the right situation presents itself and you can showcase your talents. My hat's off to [crew chief] Chad [Knaus]. We're both in a similar situation of trying to prove ourselves. I'm just blown away." Johnson added: "The resources at Hendrick Motorsports—the chassis, the bodies, the support from Lowe's [team sponsor]—it all lets us do what we need to do on the race track and not worry about anything else." Asked about a Daytona 500 front row occupied by two drivers, Johnson and Kevin Harvick, who had never started the Daytona race before, Johnson smiled and said, "Could be one heck of a wreck, couldn't it?"[13]

Johnson finished a respectable 15th in the Daytona 500. After a 28th place finish at North Carolina Speedway in

A speed of 185.831 miles per hour during qualifying earned Jimmie Johnson the pole position for the Daytona 500 on February 9, 2002.

Rockingham, North Carolina, Johnson went on a remarkable run. He collected eight consecutive top-10 finishes, culminating with his first Cup victory in his home state of California. A sixth-place finish in the season's third race at Las Vegas and a third-place finish at Atlanta Motor Speedway put him in 10th place in the points standings. He followed with a sixth-place finish at Darlington Raceway in South Carolina, a seventh-place finish at Bristol in Tennessee, and a sixth-place finish at Texas Motor Speedway. His finish in Texas elevated him to third in the points standings. At Martinsville, Virginia, he faltered with a 35th-place finish. Martinsville Speedway, one of NASCAR's pioneer tracks, takes its toll on many drivers—even veterans—because it is a tight .526 mile track. In the next race, at Talladega Superspeedway in Alabama, Johnson was back on the pole with a speed of 194.224 miles per hour. He finished seventh at Talladega.

Then it was on to California Speedway.

After qualifying fourth, Johnson led four times in the race for 62 laps. Knaus made a key decision late in the race. When the leaders of the race made pit stops on lap 234 of the 250-lap race, Knaus said Johnson's No. 48 Chevrolet would only be refueled. While the other leaders were getting either two or all four new tires put on their cars, Johnson sped out of the pits. Three laps later he passed veteran Bill Elliott, then held off Kurt Busch for the victory. It was only his 13th Cup start. Johnson crossed the finish line .620 of a second ahead of Busch. Elated by his achievement, Johnson was almost speechless. "When you get in this situation [you think] you have something to say," he said, "but you have nothing to say. You're just stoked." Later, speaking from the heart, he said, "Deep down inside, it feels really, really good to accomplish what we did. I'm just blown away."[14] Johnson left California fifth in the points chase.

Another rookie season highlight for Johnson was when he swept both races at Dover International Speedway in Delaware. He was the first Cup rookie to win both races at a track in one season. With its steep banks and concrete surface, Dover's "Monster Mile" is a difficult track even for experienced drivers. Terry Labonte has participated in 52 races at Dover, but he's yet to win there. Johnson recalled that when he raced at Dover in ASA races he was intimidated by the track because the racing speeds are high and drivers frequently are in contact with the walls:

At the time, the Milwaukee Mile was the biggest and fastest race track I had been on. It's a mile track, but it's flat. Going to Dover was just a whole new animal, something I'd never experienced before. As time goes on and you go to Daytona a couple times and

Jimmie Johnson's crew chief, Chad Knaus, can visualize what adjustments need to be made to the race car, based on Johnson's description of the car's performance on the track. The right chemistry between crew chief and driver is an essential element of a winning team.

you race at Bristol, and you go to places where your sensation of speed is really high, it really helps you get used to that and feel comfortable with your eyeballs rolling around in your head at the speed.[15]

In the first Dover event, in early June, Johnson led a race-high 188 of the 400 laps. He beat Bill Elliott again, this time by .478 of a second. Johnson said he knew early in the race that he had a fast, reliable car. Leaving Delaware's

Jimmie Johnson (No. 48) and teammate Jeff Gordon (No. 24) coming into Turn 1 at Dover International Speedway in Dover, Delaware.

capital city, Johnson was 136 points behind leader Sterling Marlin.

Johnson remained second or third in points through the next 10 races. He dropped to fifth for two races, then climbed back to third following a 13th-place finish at Richmond, Virginia. In late September, in the season's 28th of 36 races, Johnson won again at Dover. He sped across the finish line .535 of a second ahead of points leader Mark Martin. Johnson paced a race-high 170 laps, including the last 80 laps. With Martin pursuing him in the closing laps, Johnson was asked how he could stay calm. "I didn't," he said. "I'm still trying to catch my breath. I drove my butt off those last laps. Mark was on my bumper. I couldn't even see the hood of his car. All I could see was the windshield. You just keep talking to yourself."[16] Johnson wasn't worried about Martin trying any wild moves because Martin is known as a "clean" driver. After that race at Dover, Johnson was just 30 points behind Martin. When asked if he was surprised that he had a chance to win the points title, Johnson laughed and said, "Of course. You've got to be realistic. I never in my wildest dreams thought I'd be in this situation."

A 10th place finish by Johnson and a 25th by Martin in the next race at Kansas Speedway moved Johnson into first place in the points standings. He was the first rookie to lead the Cup points standings. Imagine his joy at leading the points as a rookie. "We realize the chance is there [to win the title]," he said. "We still have the same approach and the same attitude. We need to do what's gotten us to this point, which is to have fun and be fast."[17] Unfortunately for Johnson, he was unable to maintain the lead. In the season's final seven races, his best were two sixth-place finishes. Still, fifth place in the points standings was a tremendous achievement for a rookie.

Jeff Gordon, Johnson's teammate at Hendrick Motorsports and co-owner of Johnson's car, was impressed by his younger friend. "He's just a good guy," Gordon said. "He's a great guy to have on your team. He works so well with people and he can drive the wheels off [a car]."[18]

There was no "sophomore slump" for Johnson in 2003. In professional stick-and-ball sports, outstanding first seasons are frequently followed by "off" years. Opponents learn athletes' weaknesses during the first seasons and take advantage of them in later seasons. Proving how talented he is and how strong his team is, Johnson improved over his rookie year. he finished second in the standings, only 90 points behind champion Matt Kenseth. Johnson matched his rookie season

Jimmie Johnson celebrates in victory lane following the rain-shortened Coca-Cola 600 at Lowe's Motor Speedway, in Concord, North Carolina.

victory total with three wins: he collected another sweep, this time at New Hampshire International Speedway (NHIS), and also won the rain-shortened Coca-Cola 600 at Lowe's Motor Speedway in Concord, North Carolina. Following his second win of the year at NHIS's mile oval, Johnson said, "We were happy that we won and excited that we won, but the energy was so different from normal. It was just a very odd race." Johnson was referring to an accident on pit road when Jeff Gordon's car slid and struck three members of Johnson's crew. "To have those guys come so close to being seriously injured was really something," Johnson said. "It was the weirdest race for us. Even in victory lane we were all standing around looking at each other. When you see your teammates and friends come so close to being injured, it puts it all in check. For those guys to jump off the wall and do stops again with the close call they had . . . they had to overcome a lot mentally to step up and do that. [Crew chief] Chad [Knaus] could have easily lost his focus during the race. He made the right calls."[19] Prior to the next pit stop after the accident, Johnson said he could hear his crew members on the radio arguing that they wanted to continue doing their jobs and not make the mandatory trip to the infield medical center.

The Coca-Cola 600 victory was pleasing to Johnson because the year before he had been in the same position race, and he made a mistake during a pit stop. After qualifying as the fastest driver and leading 263 of the race's 400 laps he finished seventh. Only two drivers in 2003 had more wins: Ryan Newman with eight, and Kurt Busch with four. Johnson never led the points standings, but he was the only driver to stay in the top 10 for all 36 races. That consistency is how championships are won in the long run.

DID YOU KNOW?

In 2002 Jimmie Johnson and Jeff Gordon, his Hendrick Motorsports teammate, joined Colin Edwards, the World Superbike champion, to win the Race of Champions Nations Cup. The Nations Cup is an annual event that matches the world's best rally, motorcycle, and circuit racers against each other.

4

MENTORS AND MARRIAGE

When Johnson arrived in the NASCAR Cup series, he wasn't as well known as some other drivers. He had raced in California and then in the American Speed Association (ASA). Johnson wasn't a big winner in NASCAR's Busch Grand National series. From the start in the Cup series, however, Johnson impressed people with his maturity. When he spoke with the media early in his rookie season in 2002, he seemed calm but not overly confident. To be a successful racer, a person must be aggressive on the track and confident in his or her abilities. Johnson has always seemed like the type of person that people enjoy being around. After his first few successful full-time seasons in the Cup series, it was difficult to find anyone who disliked him. He is similar in makeup to Jeff Gordon, his teammate and co-owner of Johnson's car. Unlike Gordon, however, Johnson does not have a great number of NASCAR fans who boo him whenever he is introduced at races. Monte Dutton, the respected NASCAR writer, has described Johnson as "a relatively uncomplicated young man who just wants to race and has been willing to make the necessary sacrifices."[20] He misses riding

Jimmie Johnson (left) values teammate Jeff Gordon's advice on handling the business side of things, fans, and the media attention that comes with being a NASCAR driver. Gordon is co-owner of Johnson's car.

motorcycles. But he knows he can't ride motorcycles while he is racing in NASCAR. A crash on a motorcycle and the resulting injuries would cost him his Hendrick Motorsports ride and the millions he earns each year. "I truly love and enjoy [riding motorcycles]," Johnson said, "but I know if I go down, it's all over."[21]

Johnson's relationship with teammate Jeff Gordon and crew chief Chad Knaus is excellent. Johnson said of Gordon:

He has been one of the major reasons why I've been able to step into the top division of our sport and be competitive on the track. When you have somebody who is as humble and good as Jeff Gordon to learn from, it's been one of the biggest assets I could have ever hope for, [plus] driving for Hendrick Motorsports. I know I can go to Jeff and get a straight answer, even if it's a competitive advantage that might result in my beating him in the race. He's completely open and honest with me about what he's doing with the race car. It's a unique teammate situation in NASCAR.[22]

Johnson says he also tries to help Gordon whenever he can. Gordon has helped Johnson handle things off the track, like the business side, the fans, and the mental aspects of racing. Preaching patience on the track has been Gordon's major bit of advice to Johnson. Early in Johnson's rookie Cup season, Gordon reminded him that the Cup races are longer than the Busch series races. "[Gordon] said you have many opportunities to work on the car," Johnson remembered. "If you can stay on the lead lap, stay patient and keep working on the car, crazy things happen. The race turns around, comes your way and you can salvage good finishes out of bad days."[23]

Talking about why he and team owner Rick Hendrick chose Johnson, Gordon said, "I'm glad I ran those two years in the Busch series because I was able to meet Jimmie and get to know him and see him drive the race car. It appeared to me that you put this guy behind a top-notch team [in the Cup series] and he would get a lot out of it. He seemed like a smart driver."[24]

Gordon, Johnson, and their friends have spent time together away from the race tracks. Prior to the 2004 season, Gordon took Johnson on his first scuba-diving trip. After Johnson took a scuba-diving course, they headed to the Bahamas. Said Johnson: "Before I knew it, we were swimming around a ship that had sunk there. Jeff spotted a shark and then chased the shark, which I thought was a bad idea. As he is chasing the shark, it led us to probably 15 more sharks."

As Johnson thought about the underwater scene later, he was surprised how calm he was around the sharks:

> It's weird how calm you are when surrounded by one of your biggest fears. I realized there wasn't anything I could do to get away from them. If they wanted to, they would just swim over and take a bite out of me. I hung on to a rock on the bottom for a little bit and then left. I climbed out of the water basically speechless. But Jeff was high-fiving one of the guys who was with us on the dive.

Gordon laughed as he remembered the experience. "Jimmie doesn't scare easily, but I think he was pretty nervous," Gordon said. "It was a lot of fun."[25]

Johnson says Gordon has helped him to handle the media attention that successful NASCAR drivers attract. Johnson follows Gordon's advice regarding having balance in life. He has seen that Gordon manages to have a personal life and enjoy himself. "I have the network set up around me and I'm falling in line with it, and it's working great," Johnson said. "That's another advantage of driving for the team I'm driving for and having Jeff as a coach and mentor. He's found a way to stay fresh and energetic through all of this stuff."[26]

There are interesting comparisons between Johnson and Gordon's first three seasons in Cup racing. Gordon didn't win any races his first season in 1993. Two years later, he won the first of his four championships. Johnson had more victories (14) in his first three seasons than Gordon (9), but Johnson didn't earn any titles.

Knaus, a native of Rockford, Illinois, was promoted to his first crew chief job with Johnson after working at Hendrick Motorsports. He started at Hendrick in 1993 when Ray Evernham was Jeff Gordon's crew chief. Knaus later worked for Dale Earnhardt Inc. and Tyler Jet Motorsports before returning to Hendrick. When Knaus was just 14 years old, he served as his father's crew chief for a championship season at Rockford Speedway. Knaus said:

Jimmie and I were fortunate to be able to [get along] right out of the box. We had a couple of test sessions and went to some social activities before the start of the season and really clicked. You talk to some drivers and crew chiefs and they never get it to work. They don't find the right chemistry. Jimmie and I have made such big gains on our communications skills and teamwork. We can identify with whatever each other is feeling—by facial expressions or tone of voice or whatever.[27]

Johnson says the chemistry between the two has been strong from the start:

It's been one of the few relationships I've ever had in my life where I didn't have to work at having a relationship. It just kind of clicked. He doesn't need to babysit me [and] I don't have to babysit him. It's just been a good, easy working relationship. I truly believe that the driver/crew chief relationship is probably one of the most important things on the team. If you look at all the major race teams, what separates the teams? I really think it's the people. If I can't describe what the car is doing in a way that Chad can understand, we're not going to make any positive gains. Ever since the first time I was in one of his race cars and I explained what I felt on the track, he could visualize it and adjust to it. It was one of the most amazing things I've ever been a part of.

Jimmie Johnson (left) jokes around with crew chief Chad Knaus. Johnson is described as a genuine person—it's difficult to find anyone who dislikes him.

For whatever reason, Chad and I can verbalize to one another what's going on.[28]

During the 2003 season, Johnson's second year in the Cup series, Knaus said that keeping a steady pace is one of the big problems for drivers and crew chiefs. "When we win, we've got to be sure we maintain a level attitude," Knaus said. "Same when we don't do well. We can't have peaks and valleys emotionally, because that's where a lot of strain comes from. The guys on our team are still fairly young and they kind of feed on the emotion that we put out there."[29]

When it's time to race, Johnson, Knaus, and the rest of the crew are as serious as any people involved in the Cup Series.

"Once I saw her, that was pretty much the end for me." Jimmie Johnson married Chandra Janway in December of 2004.

But there's always time for a laugh. After Johnson swept the two 2004 Cup races at Pocono Raceway in Pennsylvania he collected a substantial bonus. A smiling Johnson said he would give Knaus a percentage of the money. Pretending to be offended, Knaus said that Johnson had promised him half of the bonus.

On December 11, 2004, Johnson married model Chandra Janway, of Muskogee, Oklahoma. They exchanged wedding vows on the island of St. Bart's in the Caribbean. Jeff Gordon was in the wedding party. Gordon had played matchmaker in the romance. After a friend of Johnson's introduced him to Chandra, Gordon relayed positive information about each to the other. "Once I saw her, that was pretty much the end for me," Johnson said. "Then, as I got to know her, that's when it really grabbed me. The last thing on my mind was settling down, but when I met her, it just stopped me in my tracks." After about five months, Johnson asked family and friends when a person knows he or she has met the right soulmate. All advised Johnson, "You'll know." Johnson and Chandra had dated for a year when they were snowboarding in Colorado. "I just caught her off guard on the mountain one morning," Johnson recalled. "I dropped down and proposed. It was pretty cool. I'm just so excited to start this new stage of my life. It's something I've always wanted, but I couldn't see it until I met Chani."[30]

One of the perks of being a star NASCAR driver is meeting celebrities. In 2003, Johnson was a presenter at the Country Music Television awards in Nashville. He and country music star Chris Cagle presented an award to Joe Nichols for the Breakthrough Video of the Year. Johnson has done this type of work before. For example, as a top-five finisher in the Cup points standings his first three years in the series, he was on the stage at the Waldorf-Astoria Hotel in New York City for NASCAR's annual awards dinner. Dressed in a tuxedo and speaking to a full ballroom and a national television audience, Johnson handled his duty flawlessly.

The Nashville appearance was different from that in New York City. Before the Country Music Television awards show began, Johnson spoke with Cagle, a big NASCAR fan. When it was time to go on stage, Johnson gulped and said, "I haven't been this nervous since the Daytona 500." The presentation went well and later at the VIP party, Johnson talked to several more country stars. Referring to Cagle, Johnson said, "He showed up with his NASCAR jacket on. He was

NEXTEL Cup driver Jimmie Johnson is ready for practice at Daytona National Speedway in February 2005.

talking about wanting to go to every race and play a concert for the fans on Saturday night before a race."[31]

Shortly after the start of the war in Iraq in March 2003, Lowe's, Johnson's sponsor, and the USO (United Services Organization) announced a partnership.

"I've heard of the USO, but I wasn't familiar with what the USO was about and what it did until I went through my crash course [about the organization]," Johnson said:

> I'm very proud and honored to be part of it. As I've learned about it, I understand that it's really the only support system for our troops overseas for morale and then when they get back home. The level they

go through to take care of our troops' families and even the troops in certain cases is a great cause. The package is designed to raise morale for our troops overseas. I can be a leader in some respects to show the NASCAR community and the fans that we need to support our troops. Maybe some people don't agree with the fact that we're at war. But regard-less, I think everyone agrees that we need to support our troops, and that's what this program is designed around. I want to support our troops that are defend-ing our country and keeping us free and keeping the world a safer place.[32]

Listeners could tell that Johnson really meant what he said.

Jimmie Johnson has always seemed comfort-able dealing with the busi-ness side of racing. "Racing is something that I've done since I was 5 years old. At 15, I found myself racing pro-fessionally. And I didn't have the means, through my fam-ily, for them to buy me race cars. I had to go out and meet people and talk myself into an opportunity. I had to get the job done. Maybe that programmed me for the way I handle things today."

5

IN THE EYE
OF THE STORM

Jimmie Johnson is not the kind of athlete who sparks controversy—far from it. Until the 2005 season, it was difficult to find anyone in the NASCAR garage area who disliked Johnson. He has been a "vanilla" kind of guy: pleasant, cooperative, and successful on the race track. You did not hear him criticize other drivers.

Suddenly though, as the 2005 Nextel Cup season began, Johnson was involved in controversy and disputes. First, after his car failed inspection at Las Vegas in March because the roof was too low, NASCAR deducted 25 points from him. This penalty dropped him to second in the standings, 10 points behind reigning champion Kurt Busch.

Incidents with Jeff Burton at Bristol Motor Speedway and Tony Stewart at Phoenix International Speedway followed. During the Bristol race on April 3, Johnson bumped Jeff Burton. Burton's car spun, went low, then slid up the track. Kurt Busch could not avoid hitting Burton head-on. After saying he respects Johnson, Burton said, "He's got to be better than that. He can't be doing that, and I won't put up with it."[33] At the Phoenix race on April 23, Johnson

Jeff Burton (No. 31) hit the wall after colliding with Kurt Busch (No. 97) at the Bristol Motor Speedway on April 3, 2005. Burton blamed Jimmie Johnson for causing the accident.

appeared to tap Stewart's car from behind, causing Stewart's car to spin. Stewart's car took out three other cars. "The only way you spin out like that is when a guy jacks you up like that going into (Turn) 3," Stewart said. "I don't know what he was doing. He was running guys up and down the race track. He about ran [Dale Earnhardt Jr.] into the wall."[34]

Johnson responded, "The last three or four weeks I've raced with [Tony], when I get to him he's mad that I'm going by and he starts [gesturing] and running me all over the place. I don't know why he gets so [mad] whenever I'm around him. I end up being the whipping post every time I get to him, it seems like."[35]

Prior to the next race, at Talladega Superspeedway, Johnson had cooled down. "I hate what happened, and we got together," he said. "It's just natural that after [races] everyone's emotions are high. Tony and I are great friends, and always will be."[36]

This was not the first time during the 2005 season that Johnson and Stewart had a dispute. Near the end of the Daytona 500 in February, their cars bumped after the checkered flag. In the garage area, Chad Knaus, Johnson's crew chief, and Stewart were involved in a loud argument.

After a multi-car wreck at Talladega in April, Dale Earnhardt Jr. accused Johnson of triggering the crash. Earnhardt said, "If there was an idiot out there, it was [Johnson]."[37] Johnson laughed it off, saying his wife Chandra calls him an idiot every day. Since Johnson was the points leader, the suspicion was that some of his racing rivals were trying to get inside his head. Prior to the Darlington race on Mother's Day weekend, Jeremy Mayfield, driver of the No. 19 Dodge, said:

> It started at Bristol. Jeff Burton and I were racing to-
> gether nose to tail, didn't touch each other, didn't hit
> each other. I pass Burton and the next thing I know,
> I looked in my rearview mirror and he was turned
> around. I found out later that Jimmie just punted

Dale Earnhardt Jr. accused Jimmie Johnson of triggering this 12-car crash at the Talladega Superspeedway in Talladega, Alabama, on April 30, 2005. Others passed off the growing controversy about Jimmie Johnson's aggressive driving as fuel for good newspaper stories.

[bumped] him, basically. You give a guy one [mistake] every once in a while. That's not aggressive driving.[38]

Continuing, Mayfield said:

You've got to be careful because, if you call it aggressive driving, then Jimmie is going to think he's doing everything right. [But] that's not the Dale Earnhardt aggressive driving style. Earnhardt would just nudge you and put [the car] where it was supposed to be. You didn't see him wreck everybody all the time, or whatever is going on now with Jimmie. A couple of things happened, and it looks like he's taking people out all the time.[39]

Addressing whether Johnson's tactics were receiving more attention because he was the points leader, Mayfield said:

What makes you a bigger target is when you do what you've been doing. No matter if you're the points leader or not, your target gets bigger and bigger. You've got more people shooting at your target than what you realize. To win the championship, you need to race like you've been racing, not change your ways after you become the points leader."[40]

At the next race, at Darlington Raceway in South Carolina, Mayfield said he would be looking out for Johnson. "I'll probably race him different," Mayfield said, "and it won't be the pull-over and be courteous (style). I'll just race him like he's been racing, and go from there. When that happens, everyone will start doing you that way, and you might not become the points leader anymore."[41]

Before the Darlington race, Johnson calmly dismissed the criticism. "I'm racing hard," he said. "I'm doing my job." Referring to the earlier disputes, he said, "I've gone through each of those incidents and moved on.[42] With the new rules packages things are a little bit different. The cars are a little tougher to drive. I think the competition is a little tougher than it's been."[43] Giving the issue further thought, Johnson said:

It makes me uncomfortable to hear things and to be accused of whatever it is. I know that there's a lot of fans out there that don't like me. They're wearing red [Earnhardt Jr.'s color]. I know there's a lot of fans out there wearing blue [Johnson's color] that do like me. It makes me think harder about who I am, what I am and the type of driver I am. I'm not going to let anybody's opinion change what I do or what I am.[44]

Jamie McMurray, driver of the No. 42 Dodge, was not as upset with Johnson as Earnhardt Jr. and some others. He said:

Jimmie Johnson (left) describes his car's movements to co-owner and teammate Jeff Gordon during preparations for a race at the Darlington Raceway in May 2005. Gordon has defended Johnson against recent criticism, noting that Johnson is the points leader.

Everybody has days like Jimmie had at Talladega. A couple of drivers had some harsh words about him, and it makes for a really good (newspaper) story. Jimmie is very aggressive, but a lot of drivers are that way. Maybe this year it has caught up with him a little since the deal with Tony (Stewart) happened at Phoenix and Jeff Burton at Bristol. If it was spread out over the year, it wouldn't be so bad. But because it happened in the last couple of months, it's been spotlighted a little more than usual, plus he's our points leader.[45]

Predictably, Jeff Gordon defended his Hendrick Motorsports teammate (Gordon is co-owner of Johnson's car):

> Throughout my career, I've made plenty of mistakes. I don't see how you can put the blame on any one person. I think it was just frustration coming out of Dale Earnhardt Jr. Jimmie has a great head on his shoulders, and he has a lot of support. He also has a lot riding now. He's leading in the points.[46]

NASCAR did not seem concerned about Johnson. Jim Hunter, NASCAR's vice president of corporate communication, said, "At 190 miles per hour, running inches apart, things are going to happen on a race track. I don't think Jimmie Johnson was the sole reason for that crash."[47]

As the season progressed, with Johnson either the points leader or near the top, the spotlight continued to focus on him. That goes with the territory as one of NASCAR's most talented drivers. Johnson is expected to handle this role the way he has everything else in racing—like the professional he is.

DID YOU KNOW?

Chad Knaus, Jimmie Johnson's crew chief, grew up in racing. While he was still in high school, he was crew chief for his father, a racer in the Midwest. Following graduation, Chad headed south. He began working for Hendrick Motorsports in 1993. He was a tire changer on Jeff Gordon's championship Cup teams in 1995 and '97. After working for a couple other NASCAR teams, Knaus returned to Hendrick in 2002 as Johnson's crew chief.

NOTES

Chapter 1

1. Scott Dodd, "Racing family mourns Hendrick crash victims," *Charlotte Oberver*, October 25, 2004. *www.thatsracin.com/mld/thatsracin/10006582.htm*.

2. Jimmie Johnson, press conference, October 29, 2004.

3. Jimmie Johnson, Atlanta post-race press conference, November 21, 2004.

4. Jim Hawkins, "Johnson doesn't like the points system," *The Oakland Press*, June 18, 2004. *http://theoaklandpress.com/stories/061904/pro_20040619049.shtml*.

5. Jimmie Johnson, Atlanta post-race press conference. November 21, 2004.

6. Ibid.

7. Jimmie Johnson, conference call with Bill Fleischman, February 22, 2005.

8. Jimmie Johnson, Daytona 500 post-race press conference, February 20, 2005.

Chapter 2

9. Al Levine, "Jimmie Johnson no overnight success," *Atlanta Journal Constitution*, May 2002.

10. Jenna Fryer, "Racing a family affair with the Johnsons," *Associated Press*, May 30, 2002.

11.   Ron Lemasters Jr., "Off road and on track," *Stock Car Racing*, December 1999.

12.   Jimmie Johnson, conference call with Bill Fleischman, April 22, 2003.

13.   National Association for Stock Car Racing (NASCAR) press release, May 1, 2002.

Chapter 3

14.   Jimmie Johnson, press conference, February 9, 2002.

15.   Jimmie Johnson, post-race press conference, April 28, 2002.

16.   Jimmie Johnson, conference call with Bill Fleischman, September 16, 2003.

17.   Ibid.

18.   Ibid.

19.   Jimmie Johnson, Talladega Superspeedway post-race press conference, October 1, 2002.

20.   Jeff Gordon, press conference, June 7, 2002.

21.   Jimmie Johnson, Dover Motor Speedway post-race press conference, September 16, 2003.

Chapter 4

22.   Monte Dutton, "Johnson just goes about his business . . .", *Gaston Gazette*, July 26, 2004.

23.   Ibid.

24.   Jimmie Johnson, conference call with Bill Fleischman, April 27, 2004.

25.   Jimmie Johnson, press conference, June 7, 2002.

26.   Jeff Gordon, press conference, June 7, 2002.

27.   Mike Finney, "There's no panic; Johnson cool despite dropping out of top ten," *Daytona Beach News Journal*, February 26, 2004.

28.   Ibid.

29.   Ibid.

30.   Jimmie Johnson, press conference, June 7, 2002.

31.   Chad Knaus, conference call with Bill Fleischman, September 30, 2003.

32.   Jimmie Johnson, press conference, June 7, 2002.

Chapter 5

33.   Mike Hembree, "Turn Four: Multiple wrecks litter track," *NASCAR Scene*, April 11, 2005. *http:// jimmie_johnson.scenedaily.com/stories/2005/04/11/ nextel_coverage5.html.*

34.   Jim Utter, "Stewart, Johnson add another verse as NASCAR's discordant due du jour," ThatsRacin. com, April 24, 2005. *www.thatsracin.com/mld/ thatsracin/11479029.htm.*

35.   Ibid.

36.   Jim Utter, "Johnson says spat with Stewart behind them," ThatsRacin.com, April 30, 2005. *www.*

*thatsracin.com/mld/thatsracin/sports/motorsports/
nascar/drivers/jimmie_johnson/11533368.htm.*

37.   Ed Hinton, "NASCAR says Johnson's driving not
a problem," *Orlando Sentinel*, May 6, 2005. *www.
thatsracin.com/mld/thatsracin/sports/motorsports/
nascar/drivers/jimmie_johnson/11580274.htm.*

38.   Ibid.

39.   Monte Dutton, "Darlington's not a bad place for
Johnson to put it all behind him," *Gaston Gazette*,
May 6, 2005.

40.   Ibid.

41.   Ibid.

42.   Ed Hinton, "NASCAR says Johnson's driving not a
problem."

43.   Monte Dutton, "Darlington's not a bad place for
Johnson to put it all behind him."

44.   Bob Pockrass, "Johnson shrugs off 'idiot' label from
Junior," *NASCAR Scene*, May 16, 2005. *http://
jimmie_johnson.scenedaily.com/stories/2005/05/16/
scene_circuit1.html.*

45.   Monte Dutton, "Darlington's not a bad place for
Johnson to put it all behind him."

46.   Ibid.

47.   Ed Hinton, "NASCAR says Johnson's driving not a
problem."

CHRONOLOGY

1975 Jimmie is born September 17 in El Cajon, California.

1976 Jimmie rides a "pee wee" motorcycle for the first time. A year later, he races a dirt motorcycle for the first time.

1977 Wins his first of three Mickey Thompson Stadium Truck series championships.

1994 Wins the SCORE Desert championship.

1998 Named Rookie of the Year in the American Speed Association (ASA) series.

1999 Wins two ASA races and finishes third in the points standings.

2000 In his rookie season in the Busch Grand National series, Jimmie finishes 10th in points.

2001 Makes his Cup series debut, driving for Hendrick Motorsports, at Lowe's Motor Speedway in Concord, North Carolina. He finishes 39th after qualifying 15th fastest.

2002 In his first full season in the Cup series, he wins his first race at California Speedway in his native state. Finishes an impressive fifth in the Cup points standings.

2003 Jimmie wins three Cup races and finishes second in the points standings.

2004 He is runner-up again in points, trailing champion Kurt Busch by just eight points. Jimmie wins a series-leading eight races, including four of the last six.

STATISTICS

Jimmie Johnson

Year	Races	Wins	Top 5	Top 10	Poles	Rank	Money Won
2001	3	0	0	0	0	52	$122,320
2002	36	3	6	21	4	5	$3,788,268
2003	36	3	14	20	2	2	$7,745,530
2004	36	8	20	23	1	2	$8,226,761
Total	**111**	**14**	**40**	**64**	**7**		**$19,922,879**

2003 Race Results

Race	Start	Finish
Daytona Beach, Florida	10	3
Rockingham, North Carolina	37	8
Las Vegas, Nevada	10	11
Hampton, Georgia	11	32
Darlington, South Carolina	14	27
Bristol, Tennessee	23	8
Fort Worth, Texas	4	8
Dry Valley, Alabama	7	15
Martinsville, Virginia	7	9
Fontana, California	20	16
Richmond, Virginia	10	19
Concord, North Carolina	**37**	**1**
Dover, Delaware	5	38
Long Pond, Pennsylvania	1	12
Brooklyn, Michigan	11	16
Sonoma, California	37	17
Daytona Beach, Florida	11	18
Joliet, Illinois	6	3

Loudon, New Hampshire	**6**	**1**
Long Pond, Pennsylvania	2	15
Indianapolis, Indiana	9	18
Watkins Glen, New York	20	4
Brooklyn, Michigan	15	27
Bristol, Tennessee	16	5
Darlington, South Carolina	2	3
Richmond, Virginia	26	11
Loudon, New Hampshire	**8**	**1**
Dover, Delaware	4	8
Dry Valley, Alabama	3	34
Kansas City, Kansas	1	7
Concord, North Carolina	3	3
Martinsville, Virginia	26	2
Hampton, Georgia	9	3
Phoenix, Arizona	3	2
Rockingham, North Carolina	18	2
Homestead, Florida	10	3

Points standing: 2nd

2004 Race Results

Race	Start	Finish
Daytona Beach, Florida	6	5
Rockingham, North Carolina	29	41
Las Vegas, Nevada	12	16
Hampton, Georgia	3	4
Darlington, South Carolina	**11**	**1**
Bristol, Tennessee	11	16
Fort Worth, Texas	8	9
Martinsville, Virginia	8	4

Dry Valley, Alabama	8	4
Fontana, California	19	2
Richmond, Virginia	5	2
Concord, North Carolina	**1**	**1**
Dover, Delaware	14	32
Long Pond, Pennsylvania	**5**	**1**
Brooklyn, Michigan	3	4
Sonoma, California	34	5
Daytona Beach, Florida	19	2
Joliet, Illinois	3	2
Loudon, New Hampshire	2	11
Long Pond, Pennsylvania	**14**	**1**
Indianapolis, Indiana	9	36
Watkins Glen, New York	1	40
Brooklyn, Michigan	1	40
Bristol, Tennessee	11	3
Fontana, California	16	14
Richmond, Virginia	3	36
(Chase for the Championship)		
Loudon, New Hampshire	2	11
Dover, Delaware	9	10
Dry Valley, Alabama	16	37
Kansas City, Kansas	4	32
Concord, North Carolina	**9**	**1**
Martinsville, Virginia	**18**	**1**
Hampton, Georgia	**8**	**1**
Phoenix, Arizona	13	6
Darlington, South Carolina	**4**	**1**
Homestead, Florida	39	2

Points standing: 2nd

Jimmie Johnson is not car No. 48's first driver in the Cup series, but Johnson holds the best record for that car.

Year	Driver	Rank
2005	Jimmie Johnson	1
2004	Jimmie Johnson	2
2203	Jimmie Johnson	2
2002	Jimmie Johnson	5
2001	Jimmie Johnson	52
1993	Trevor Boys	79
1993	James Hylton	64
1992	James Hylton	42
1991	James Hylton	54
1990	James Hylton	107
1990	Ben Hess	89
1990	Freddie Crawford	108
1989	Greg Sacks	32
1989	Mickey Gibbs	41
1987	Jerry Holden	106
1987	Tony Spanos	109
1987	James Hylton	80
1986	Ron Esau	114
1986	Ken Ragan	40
1986	Johnny Coy Jr.	74
1986	Trevor Boys	34
1986	Jerry Cranmer	55
1986	James Hylton	58
1986	Ronnie Thomas	44
1986	Morgan Shepherd	18
1986	Ronnie Slark	116
1986	Eddie Bierschwale	24

1984	Trevor Boys	17
1983	Trevor Boys	25
1983	Lennie Pond	34
1983	James Hylton	61
1982	D.K. Ulrich	24
1982	Lennie Pond	33
1982	James Hylton	28
1982	Tommy Gale	21
1982	Slick Johnson	29
1981	James Hylton	19
1981	Harry Gant	3
1980	James Hylton	13
1980	Dan Gurney	122
1979	James Hylton	14
1978	James Hylton	26
1978	Al Holbert	34
1978	Walter Ballard	97
1978	Hershel McGriff	84
1977	James Hylton	7
1976	James Hylton	13
1975	James Hylton	3

FURTHER READING

Dutton, Monte. *At Speed: Up Close & Personal With The People, Places & Fans of NASCAR*. Dulles, VA: Brasseys, Inc., 2000.

Hawkins, Jim. *Tales From The Daytona 500*. Champaign, IL: Sports Publishing, 2003.

Hembree, Michael. *NASCAR: The Definitive History of America's Sport*. New York, NY: Harper Entertainment, 2000.

Higgins, Tom. *NASCAR's Greatest Races: The 25 Most Thrilling Races in NASCAR History*. New York, NY: Harper Entertainment, 1999.

Pearce, Al and Bill Fleischman. *The Unauthorized NASCAR Fan Guide 2004*. Detroit, MI: Visible Ink Press, 2004.

Poole, David. *Race With Destiny: The Year That Changed NASCAR Forever*. Kingston, RI: Moyer Bell Ltd., 2004.

BIBLIOGRAPHY

Dodd, Scott. "Racing family mourns Hendrick crash victims." *Charlotte Oberver*, October 25, 2004. *www.
thatsracin.com/mld/thatsracin/10006582.htm.*

Dutton, Monte. "Darlington's not a bad place for Johnson to
put it all behind him." *Gaston Gazette*, May 6, 2005.

———. "Johnson just goes about his business . . ." *Gaston
Gazette*, July 26, 2004.

Finney, Mike. "There's no panic; Johnson cool despite
dropping out of top ten." *Daytona Beach News Journal*,
February 26, 2004.

Fryer, Jenna. "Racing a family affair with the Johnsons."
Associated Press, May 30, 2002.

Gordon, Jeff. Press conference, June 7, 2002.

Hawkins, Jim. "Johnson doesn't like the points system."
The Oakland Press, June 18, 2004. *http://
theoaklandpress.com/stories/061904/pro_20040619049.
shtml.*

Hembree, Mike. "Turn Four: Multiple wrecks litter track."
NASCAR Scene, April 11, 2005. *http://jimmie_johnson.
scenedaily.com/stories/2005/04/11/nextel_coverage5.
html.*

Hinton, Ed. "NASCAR says Johnson's driving not a problem." *Orlando Sentinel*, May 6, 2005. *www.thatsracin.*

com/mld/thatsracin/sports/motorsports/nascar/drivers/ jimmie_johnson/11580274.htm.

Johnson, Jimmie. Atlanta post-race press conference, November 21, 2004.

———. Conference call with Bill Fleischman, April 22, 2003.

———. Conference call with Bill Fleischman, April 27, 2004.

———. Conference call with Bill Fleischman, February 22, 2005.

———. Conference call with Bill Fleischman, September 16, 2003.

———. Daytona 500 post-race press conference, February 20, 2005.

———. Dover Motor Speedway post-race press conference, September 16, 2003.

———. Post-race press conference, April 28, 2002.

———. Press conference, February 9, 2002.

———. Press conference, June 7, 2002.

———. Press conference, October 29, 2004.

———. Talladega Superspeedway post-race press conference, October 1, 2002.

Knaus, Chad. Conference call with Bill Fleischman, September 30, 2003.

Lemasters Jr., Ron. "Off road and on track." *Stock Car Racing*, December 1999.

Levine, Al. "Jimmie Johnson no overnight success." *Atlanta Journal Constitution*, May 2002.

National Association for Stock Car Racing (NASCAR) press release, May 1, 2002.

Pockrass, Bob. "Johnson shrugs off 'idiot' label from Junior." *NASCAR Scene*, May 16, 2005. *http://jimmie_johnson.scenedaily.com/stories/2005/05/16/scene_circuit1.html.*

Utter, Jim. "Johnson says spat with Stewart behind them." ThatsRacin.com, April 30, 2005. *www.thatsracin.com/mld/thatsracin/sports/motorsports/nascar/drivers/jimmie_johnson/11553368.htm.*

———. "Stewart, Johnson add another verse as NASCAR's discordant due du jour." ThatsRacin.com, April 24, 2005. *www.thatsracin.com/mld/thatsracin/11479029.htm.*

ADDRESSES

NASCAR
P.O. Box 2875
Daytona Beach, FL 32120
(386) 253-0611

Jimmie Johnson
c/o Hendrick Motorsports
4400 Papa Joe Hendrick Blvd.
Charlotte, NC 28262
(704) 455-0326

INTERNET SITES

www.lowesracing.com

> *This site offers updated information on the No. 48 race team.*

www.gospeedwayworld.com/FanClub/JJ.pdf

> *A site where fans can apply to join Jimmie Johnson's fan club.*

www.nascar.com

> *This site provides information about the top three NASCAR racing series: Nextel Cup, Busch Grand National and Craftsman Truck series.*

Photo Credits:

INDEX

ABOUT THE AUTHOR

Bill Fleischman is a veteran *Philadelphia Daily News* sports writer. He has covered auto racing, college basketball, the National Hockey League and tennis. He is co-author of *The Unauthorized NASCAR Fan Guide 2004*. He is former president of the Philadelphia Sports Writers Association and the Professional Hockey Writers Association. He is an adjunct professor in the University of Delaware journalism program. A graduate of Gettysburg College, Fleischman and his wife, Barbara, live in Wilmington, Delaware.